Praise for

WHEN HOPE IS TRIED

"Ms. Winters is honest and forthright, sharing her experiences with grace and sincerity as her life with extended illness unfolds. She provides dignity in the midst of the indignity of extended illness and its treatments and shows us the beauty and redemption that can come from suffering."

—CHRISTINE O'KEEFFE LAFSER,
author, *An Empty Cradle, A Full Heart*

"Winters writes from the heart of her own journey through suffering and provides hope for others who are bewildered. Serious illness scatters our sensibilities. Winters reorders our lives in the certain knowledge of God's love."

—JOHN H. TIMMERMAN,
author, *Waiting for the Saviour, A Season of Suffering,* and
Do We Still Need the Ten Commandments?

"[Carol Winters] embraces the truths of God in such a personal and meaningful way. This inspirational book is about discovering God's greater love, power, goodness, and hope. It helps make sense out of suffering and reaches deep into the soul."

—PATTY McGINNIS,
director of Women's Ministry, Calvary Church, Grand Rapids, Michigan

When Hope Is Tried is a book for those of us who stand waiting and willing to support our friends and loved ones as they endure a difficult illness. In these meditations, readers will witness Carol's pain and embrace her faith. This book does not promise a happy journey, but it does offer hope along the way.

—NANCY HULL,
assistant professor of English, Calvin College

"As a relatively new pilgrim on the road of terminal illness, this book is a godsend. I felt Carol was speaking to me at the deepest possible level— soul to soul. I cried and laughed as I read. But most of all, I gained perspective on my own disease and found great encouragement and hope!"

—DR. EDWARD DOBSON,
senior pastor, Calvary Church, Grand Rapids, Michigan

"Carol's writing forces a person to ask deep and difficult questions about human suffering. She not only points her readers to the larger redemptive purpose in suffering—she takes us there. Painful, disturbing, and yet ultimately hopeful, this book takes faith out of the abstract and into the doctor's office."

—ROB BELL,
lead pastor, Mars Hill Bible Church

"Carol Winters's book is both amazing and searing: I learned something about the journey of a cancer patient from the inner, meditative person. And I learned, as well, about the difficulties and the elations of a Christian struggling with both illness and faith. This is a beautiful, honest book."

—PATRICIA CLARK, PH.D.,
poet-in-residence and associate professor of English, Grand Valley State University

WHEN HOPE IS TRIED

WHEN HOPE IS TRIED

Meditations for Those Who Are Ill and the People Who Love Them

CAROL WINTERS

May the God whom you see on these pages encircle you Life with this love and your guidance —

Carol Winters

LOYOLAPRESS.
CHICAGO

LOYOLAPRESS.

3441 N. ASHLAND AVENUE

Credits continued on p.129

Cover design by Elizabeth A. Sweeney/KTK Design
Cover image © Michael McGovern/Nonstock
Author photo by Patty McGinnis
Interior design by John Scapes/KTK Design

Library of Congress Cataloging-in-Publication Data

Winters, Carol, 1944–
    When hope is tried : meditations for those who are ill and the people
who love them / Carol Winters.
      p. cm.
    ISBN 0-8294-1686-2
    1.Cancer—Patients—Religious life. 2. Cancer—Religious aspects—
Christianity—Meditations. I. Title.

BV4910.33 .W56 2001
242'.4—dc21   2001029412

Printed in the United States of America
01 02 03 04 05 PhoenH 10 9 8 7 6 5 4 3 2 1

To Tom Winters, my dear and loving husband:

"We pray for a miracle, and if that doesn't come,
we take the next step."

CONTENTS

TRUST

RESOURCES

Acknowledgments

One never writes alone. Rather, writing involves many people whose enthusiasm and interest are essential for a project's completion. I want to thank Vinita Hampton Wright for her ability to see possibilities in rough draft; Heidi Hill, whose careful reading and suggestions were invaluable; and Rebecca Johnson, whose perseverance, good humor, and attention to detail were remarkable. I also want to thank my family and friends, who with unflagging patience read multiple drafts and then offered worthwhile insights. Most of all, I want to thank my husband, whose steady encouragement made me believe I could write.

*Like water spilled on the ground, which cannot be recovered,
so we must die.*

—2 Samuel 14:14 (NIV)

*The last of the freedoms: to choose one's attitude in a given
set of circumstances.*

—Viktor Frankl

Introduction

*T*hese meditations reflect a six-year period of my living with cancer. As you know from living with your own illness or from standing by someone who is ill, lessons learned have to be relearned and disappointments have to be dealt with anew each time they occur.

All the meditations are based on my personal experiences. Taken together, they depict a movement from anger to trusting God, not the circumstances. We Christians sometimes refuse to acknowledge our anger, not realizing that God can not only deal with our anger but isn't afraid of our clenched fists. He rewards honesty, and if we can turn toward him, he will transform our anger and allow us to experience glimpses of grace. We can then begin to move outside ourselves and see others as individuals who are equally important to God. We can see our situations not as roadblocks to accomplishing our real desires but as opportunities to find our real desires in glorifying God. And we can learn to trust that God loves us more than we can fathom, that he has good plans for us, and that he will see us through our lives here. The entire journey becomes one of grace—an awareness that everything is ruled by God.

I was diagnosed with stage-three breast cancer in January of 1995. I chose to undergo tram-flap surgery, a mastectomy that uses tissue from the stomach to make a new breast. The doctors also ordered chemotherapy.

In 1997, the cancer metastasized to a rib that was then radiated. However, that didn't stop the spread of the cancer; it moved through my ribs, spine, and leg. We tried several rounds of radiation and different chemotherapies, which didn't eradicate the disease but slowed its progress.

In 1999, the cancer moved to my other breast, which was then surgically removed. But the cancer moved again in 2000, this time to my chest wall and my brain. Now, radiation has reduced the brain lesions, and various drugs have stabilized the bone and chest wall sites.

SHOCK

$\mathcal{M}$E?

That's why we can be so sure that every detail in our lives of love for God is worked into something good.

ROMANS 8:28*

This used to be my least favorite verse in the Bible. Somebody always seemed to be cramming it down my throat not only when I was younger but also when I was first diagnosed with breast cancer. We call such statements platitudes, and while I know that they stem from truths—ones so overused, in fact, that they have become commonplace—hearing them doesn't help. They are most annoying when they come from people whose worst trials are a husband ruining dinner by coming home late from work, or a child biting the birthday boy at his own party, or a Bible-school worker deciding

---

* The Bible version used in this book, Eugene H. Peterson's *The Message*, does not use verse numbers, so we have added the corresponding verse numbers from traditional Scripture.

to back out at the last minute. All of these things have happened to me, and frankly, I don't remember quoting Romans 8:28 to myself then either.

When someone untouched by illness dared to quote that verse at me, it was all I could do to keep from shouting, "What do you know about anything? Wait until the doctors sit you down for 'a little talk.'"

But my mother would have been proud—I managed to restrain myself. Mostly I ignored the verse and just smiled wanly at the speaker. I didn't say, "Oh, I know, good comes in many forms" or "I don't know what the Lord's up to, but I'll trust him." I grimly clenched my teeth and said nothing as I took the cure the doctors had planned. I think I was numb after the first cancer surgery and treatment because people often quoted that verse to me.

I led a full life before I was diagnosed with stage-three breast cancer. In one week's time, I went from being a university professor who loved doling out advice to my pre-service English teachers to a patient in line for tram-flap surgery.

Before I was diagnosed, I believed that illness was just a random happening, much like being on the wrong side of town and missing that desperately needed train. I took comfort in the fact that God hadn't planned cancer for me, that he loved me too much to cause such a thing to happen. Of course, once I learned of my illness, my theory didn't seem to hold. I was left with questions of where illness came from, but I wasn't ready to deal with them yet. When the cancer reasserted itself, I had to resign myself to seemingly never-ending cycles of radiation and chemo. If I thought about that verse at all, I stood befuddled at God's definition of good.

Mainly, I refused to think about it at all. If I did, I would be forced to admit that I was angry with God. Why did this have to happen to me? I tithed, worked in the nursery, taught Sunday school, ran daily vacation Bible schools, and took notes during my pastor's sermons. Weren't there other, less religious people who needed the lessons of illness?

Lord, what's going on? How am I supposed to believe this will work out for the good? Why me? Doesn't all my work for you earn me some sort of preferential treatment?

For personal study: Genesis 37:2–10, 16–28; 45:4–5
Joseph discovers the wisdom of God's plan.

Facing Temptation

Oh, that my steps might be steady,
*   keeping to the course you set;*
Then I'd never have any regrets
*   in comparing my life with your counsel.*
I thank you for speaking straight from your heart;
*   I learn the pattern of your righteous ways.*
I'm going to do what you tell me to do;
*   don't ever walk off and leave me.*

PSALM 119:5–8

*C*hemo was worse than I could have imagined, although I had certainly heard enough about it from my predecessors. The first time I entered the falsely cheerful room where the treatment was administered and sat in one of its baby-blue Barcoloungers, I balked. Like deployed oxygen masks in an airplane cabin, IV bags filled the room, hooked up to people in various stages and kinds of treatment. Some people slept covered with white flannel sheets so that only their bald heads were showing, some talked to their neighbors or to the people who had brought them, some scowled, some smiled, some had simply vacated their bodies for the time.

The treatment itself was scary. First, I needed an IV. The nurse who came over was kind and gentle, but having her search with a needle for a juicy vein was not my idea of a good way to spend an afternoon. Once the IV was started, the first drip was for nausea; yes, I would probably get sick. Then, ugly neon-colored drugs were mainlined into my veins. The nurses, still smiling, did their best to act as if this were just another shot. However, when I read the list of side effects, I knew better. This stuff would make me retch. It would make my hair fall out, my throat bleed, and my intestines do unspeakable things. And on top of everything else, it would throw me into menopause.

My husband and I sat across from each other, quietly crying and trying to keep our tears hidden. We would steal glances at each other, wondering when we could trust ourselves to speak. I was tempted to simply stand up, rip out the IV needle, and run. But, of course, I didn't.

Dietrich Bonhoeffer tells us that the psalms were Christ's prayers. In Psalm 119:4–6, Jesus asks the Father to keep him steadfast in obedience, able to learn the laws of God, and not forsaken. I always thought Jesus was perfect, sinless, and he was, but I never considered how he got that way or maintained it. How did he feel when the devil tempted him? His body had to have been screaming for food after going without it for forty days. He had to have felt compelled by the promise of power when the devil offered him dominion over the world. And he had to have deliberated for a while once he realized that he could accept the spiritual power by deceiving himself that he would use it to glorify God.

The Scriptures make obedience look so easy—temptation in one verse, Christ's perfect response in the next. The fact that he used Scripture to deny the temptations tells me that he spent time studying it and turning little things over to God so that he would be ready to turn his whole life over to his heavenly Father. I used to think that his perfection was a gift from God. Now I see that he had to walk each day with God. He had to give over his uncertainties about life to his Father—oh, yes, he was fully human when he walked here. Jesus' sufferings came out of his humanity. Although he didn't have full knowledge when he was here, he faithfully followed God's commands.

*Lord, help me through my anger so that I, with Christ,
can meet temptations in a way that would please you.
I know that the process will take as long as I choose.
Help me to see the urgency of the situation.*

For personal study: Matthew 4:1–11

Jesus successfully meets Satan's temptations.

Help Me Understand

Get me out of here—your love is so great!—
  I'm at the end of my rope, my life in ruins.
I'm fading away to nothing, passing away,
  my youth gone, old before my time.

Psalm 109:21–24

The woman's daughter pushed her in a wheelchair to the chair next to mine. The patient was dressed in a baby-pink warm-up suit topped off with a perfect, short blond curly wig. But her careful attention to appearance belied the vacant expression on her face. She talked little and sat slumped in her chair, just waiting for chemo to start and then be over. Her sister, daughter, grandson, and granddaughter had come with her.

Her sister pulled up a chair beside her and chatted to me. Her daughter, with a disgruntled expression on her face, sat down in a wheelchair across the room from her mother. Her grandson and granddaughter, after helping their grandmother get settled in her lounge, sat down in another corner of the room. Throughout all this activity, the woman sat grim faced, staring into space, willing herself not to be there. At one point, she made it clear that she wanted to leave because the nurses weren't doing anything for her. The family quieted her down and then sat stonily waiting for the blood counts to come back. The counts didn't come while I was there that day, and my impression of the entire family is that, yes, they would endure because they were tough people, but they wouldn't smile doing it. They were angry at having to be there.

During my first round of chemo, I didn't do much better. Of course, I didn't have the entourage, because I didn't want my loved ones or friends to see me in such straits. Nor did I have the vacant look. But like the woman that day, I was silent, and I was plenty angry to be on chemo. I remember being incensed at a patient one day, an old woman. She pointed at me and asked the nurse why I still had hair while she had none. I didn't have hair; I had a wig, and I nastily guessed at what the old woman would say if I whipped off my wig and said, "Satisfied? Now I'm just as pathetic as you are."

I was also impatient if I had to wait for a nurse to get my IV started. After all, didn't appointment times mean anything to these people? And I was just plain furious if the first nurse couldn't get the needle in my arm after two tries and had to call for another nurse. Didn't they have enough empathy to know that IVs hurt? In the verse from Psalm 109, David alternately rails at God for not rescuing him and pleads with God to rescue him. When I read these verses, it's easy to see why David needs to ask for God's help; the wicked are after him. But I have trouble understanding why the wicked are after *me*. Somehow it's easier to read about someone else's crises than to live my own.

Lord, help me out of this. I know you don't want bad things for your children, but I don't understand what you do want.

For personal study: 2 Kings 5:1–15

Naaman learns obedience.

God, Where Are You?

Human life is a struggle, isn't it?
  It's a life sentence to hard labor.
Like field hands longing for quitting time
  and working stiffs with nothing to hope for but payday,
I'm given a life that meanders and goes nowhere—
  months of aimlessness, nights of misery!
I go to bed and think, "How long till I can get up?"
  I toss and turn as the night drags on—and I'm fed up!

Job 7:1–4

*T*he Bible doesn't speculate on what keeps Job awake, but every person with a long-lasting illness knows. In an effort to get comfortable, Job changes positions and inevitably knocks open a sore that has just formed a scab, or rolls onto a side that can't support all that body pressure anymore, or lies on an arm that falls asleep, and screams to be waken up.

That's what his body is doing, but what about his mind? The Bible is silent on the subject. I spend my nights asking hundreds of questions: What will my husband do when I'm dead? Who should be given that ruby-and-diamond ring? How many people will show up for my funeral? What if I can't get out of bed, shower, and get myself dressed tomorrow? And who'll then shop for groceries, do the laundry, and put the garden to sleep for the winter? God, you promised you'd be with me. Where are you?

When Job looks back on his life, he uses some telling metaphors to illuminate his feelings. He sees himself pressed into hard labor. It is the relentlessness of the illness that becomes hard to bear. Like the body that endures hard physical labor, the body that endures extended illness becomes exhausted, making every effort difficult. Even something as simple as bending down to retrieve a mitten that has fallen under a restaurant table becomes a daunting task. Lifting my twenty-month-old grandson into his car seat, not only hefting his weight but also twisting my back to position him properly, is nearly impossible.

Just as my body is strained by all this physical labor, my mind becomes dulled and skitters from one shallow topic to the next. Sustained thought becomes impossible because the body's clamor is all consuming. The disease orders you around: it decides when you'll rest and when you won't; it looks down on you as a subhuman who doesn't deserve a rich, full, and free life; it can surprise you with downturns whenever it pleases and delights in threatening to do so.

Lord, give my mind and my body some rest.
All the day-to-day details of life are overwhelming me.
Will I ever be able to return to my life?

For personal study: 1 Kings 18:19–39
Elijah shows the power of God.

GOOD INTENTIONS

Three of Job's friends heard of all the trouble that had fallen on him. . . . Then they sat with him on the ground. Seven days and nights they sat there without saying a word.

JOB 2:11, 13

*J*ob's friends came and sat beside him, horrified at his condition. They kept silent for seven whole days and just wept with him. Our friends send cards and flowers, make "cheer-up" phone calls, and drop off casseroles— anything to assure themselves that you're still alive.

Job's friends could have stopped with their quiet support; our friends could too. But they just can't. I remember the friend who met me in the center aisle of church the first Sunday I was back after surgery and asked, "Carol, did they get it all?" in tones loud enough for those sitting on either side of the aisle to hear. I stared at her for a moment, dumbfounded at her lack of sensitivity, and whispered, "I sure hope so."

I also remember the friend who stopped me downstairs at church and recounted her uncle's "long and valiant battle with cancer." Of course, he had lost that battle just last winter. I numbly murmured an "I'm sorry," backed by a quick retreat. There was the friend who asked, "Carol, just how many lymph nodes were involved?" and another one who said, "Are you going to lose your hair?" When I answered, "Yes," she replied, "Oh, isn't that a pity. And you have such thick, beautiful hair." One friend analyzed, "I think you may be in denial." I didn't have a reply for her outrageous comment, but I thought to myself, *Follow me around for a week and you'll see I'm not in denial.* In a phone call, a friend said, "Buy my vitamins, and then the cancer won't return." And finally, one friend dared to ask, "What's the prognosis?" I responded with a bleak "I'd rather not talk about it."

One woman had been diagnosed with breast cancer five months before me, and every time she saw me she would tell me what terror was just ahead in my treatment. She gave me firsthand reports on the nausea, body aches, fatigue, and terror of being constantly stuck with needles.

Unlike Job, who argued with his friends, I just avoided as many of mine as I could. It was difficult for me to talk about my condition, let alone speculate on what might be ahead. Friends would have done better to simply ask, "How are you?" If I wanted to talk, I could answer at length; if I didn't, I could answer with a polite "fine" and have a graceful way out.

Job's friends came right out and accused him of unrighteous acts; mine only hinted at such lapses. Or they noted what a blessing I could be to others. Didn't they get it? I didn't want to be a blessing. I didn't want to have cancer.

Lord, let me understand that people don't really know what to say, and so they sometimes stumble and say something hurtful. Help me to remember that their intentions are good even if they are not thought out.

For personal study: Job 11:1-6

Zophar reprimands Job.

Listening with a Loving Heart

The fears in our hearts kept us on pins and needles. We couldn't relax because we didn't know how it would turn out. Then the God who lifts up the downcast lifted our heads and our hearts with the arrival of Titus.

2 Corinthians 7:5–6

*T*he cancer came back again. The notice was a gnawing pain in my upper left leg. I tried to think it was arthritis. After all, I was certainly at the age for that problem. I spent two weeks ignoring the facts that the limp was getting worse and Tylenol hardly touched the pain. When I finally called the doctor, I thought I knew what I was in for. I did the bone scan just before we went out of town for the weekend. When we got home and heard the doctor's voice on the answering machine urging me to call his office as soon as possible, I knew for certain that I was in for trouble. Why, then, when we went in and I heard him say the words, was I surprised? Why did I cry? Fear is the only answer I can come up with. Fear of the unknown but also fear of the known. Radiation and chemo for sure, I thought. But no, radiation only this time.

When the radiation oncologist talked to me, he allayed my major fear—that my leg bone would simply snap. I had just read in the Sunday paper about that happening to a woman. But the cancer had not yet eaten through the bone, so he was hopeful that he could completely mend my limp and heal my pain. Casually, he added that sometimes the doctor would just pin the bone in order to stop a break before it happened. Immediately, images of pins in all the places I had bone cancer crowded into my head—spine, several ribs, leg. I would never get through an airport scanner again!

My mind raced in a thousand directions as I sped home, called my sister, and spilled my poison on her day. As always, she didn't cry, she didn't melt into hysterics, she didn't question, she didn't offer platitudes. She simply listened, took it all in, and played it back to me. Her calm, loving reception of my news made it bearable for me.

*Lord, thank you for the understanding of my sister,
which helps alleviate my fear. Her sensitivity reminds me
that there are many things we can do for the sick—mainly,
that we can listen with a loving heart.*

For personal study: Psalm 61:1–8
God listens to David with love.

Hollow Words

Old friends avoid me like the plague.
My cousins never visit,
   my neighbors stab me in the back.
My competitors blacken my name,
   devoutly they pray for my ruin.

PSALM 38:11–12

*E*very ill person has had the experience of friends dropping away. I don't know if they're afraid they'll have to listen to our tales of woe or if they're simply afraid to be around us.

One friend used to meet me often for lunch or dinner but was suddenly too busy. I started to wonder about it the day she passed on my invitation to lunch, claiming that she was turning her lunch hour into a business meeting. I watched her table during lunch, but I didn't see the other party appear.

Another friend would sweetly bend toward me to say, "Hi! How are you doing?" and then she would airily bounce across the room before I could reply. Two other friends never acknowledged my abrupt departure from work. Another friend wondered aloud in a departmental meeting if I would ever be well enough to teach again. Meanwhile, she knew someone who could do my job. These "friends" didn't phone, drop a note, stop by the house—they simply disappeared from my life.

So the hugs dried up, the invitations to lunch thinned out, but the words remained the same: "I'm so sorry this has happened to you; if you ever need anything just call." "I hope things go well for you. Just call if . . ." "I will pray for you. Remember to call if . . ." These were fine words that sounded reassuring to the speakers' ears, but when it came down to it, they were hollow words.

"Could you take me to radiation next week?"

"Where?"

"Downtown."

"How long are the appointments?"

"Anywhere from one to three hours, depending on the machine's mood that day and the number of emergency patients who are taken first."

"How often do you have to go for treatments?"

"Every day, but I'm just asking for one week. Actually, I have six weeks of these treatments."

"Oh, I'm sorry, but I just don't have that kind of time. I wish I could help, but call me if . . ."

Actually, I didn't have that kind of time either.

Lord, I need help dealing with insincere people who don't even know they're insincere. I'd like to just tell them how phony they are. Maybe that would get rid of some of my anger, but that's probably not what you have in mind.

For personal study: Job 19:21–26

Job pleads with his friends for pity, but then understands that he must stand on his own integrity.

GLIMPSES OF
GRACE

Faithful Friends

Friends love through all kinds of weather.

PROVERBS 17:17

I am blessed to have three best friends who not only pray for me but who also treat me as if I'm a person and not a disease. They are not constantly asking me how I am, when my next round of tests will be, what the doctor said when the cancer metastasized again. I appreciate their normalcy so much. They assume that I want to go to dinner and don't preface their request with "You aren't nauseous, are you?" Sometimes I am, and I'm sure they probably know it, especially when I leave half a portion of home-cooked pasta on my plate. The next time we have lunch they offer to split a portion or refuse to comment on my request for tea only. At one luncheon, I had ordered soup, eaten it, and then realized my stomach was about to revolt. I excused myself, dashed to the bathroom, found it locked, dashed into the men's bathroom, and let go of my lunch. When I returned, no one asked me where I had gone in such a hurry or if I had been unable to read the sign clearly marked "Men's." They simply smiled, caught me up on the conversation, and let me back into their circle.

They assume I'm still capable of teaching and ask me for my opinions on books in our field and for my advice when they're putting together conference proposals. They ask me to cover a class when they're in a pinch or offer to cover one of mine when I need help. Once, when I had to have surgery in the middle of the term, my friend came out to the university and taught a three-hour seminar for me with ease. She even praised my good organizational skills, even though I knew it was an exaggeration.

My friends assume I can still laugh at myself as well as at other people. If I forget to bring the book we're discussing to our literary meeting, they don't automatically think that my disease is on the march again. They remember times when they too have forgotten such an important part of a meeting.

And when I am sick, dragging around on painkillers, the invitations to lunch still come, the discussions about books and teaching continue, and their insistence that life go on as it has in the past is a bright spot in my day.

Lord, I thought I had been thankful for good friends in earlier years, but now I know what it means to have someone care for you. Thank you for such faithful friends.

For personal study: 1 Thessalonians 4:9–10;
Proverbs 17:17; Proverbs 18:24
Good friends are truly a blessing.

The Ugly Truth

The hot temper of a fool eventually kills him,
  the jealous anger of a simpleton does her in.

Job 5:2

*J*ob sits on his ash heap, covered with painful sores, having lost everything but his nagging wife. The disparity between his situation and his friend Eliphaz's nice life must have struck him as he listened to his friend pontificate. I confess to envying my friends, with their lovely, seemingly trouble-free lives intact—new houses, exotic trips, settled children, easy jobs. While I lived with cancer, they built new houses, their primary concern being whether or not the architect could get his discount on the California leaded glass that reigned supreme. They debated weighty questions like "Can we really do justice to Egypt, Greece, *and* Turkey in two short weeks?" They lived with such heartaches as that caused by a child who had moved to the big city or out west in order to become independent. They had begun to stay home, calling in to the office to delegate responsibility to their new, eager assistant.

I didn't quite wish trouble on them. Maybe just a small fire to take away a treasured collection, or a slight downturn in the economy so that extras had to be cut that particular year, or a child who didn't get that promotion, or a tiny readjustment in the corporate structure—any of these would have been a good spiritual happening for my friends. I thought I wasn't guilty of jealousy, but it occurs to me now that I thought this not because of any inherent loveliness on my part but because my life was sweet too, complete with new houses and fun.

While I'm confessing, I might as well say that I'm even envious of other people's diagnoses. It's not that I would have wanted my friend to have a tram flap with high lymph-node involvement like I had, but I wouldn't have minded a lumpectomy and radiation like she had either. Proverbs 14:30 says, "A heart at peace gives life to the body, but envy rots the bones." Intellectually I know that's true. But my bones are already rotting; how much can envy add to that? Now that my material securities and luxuries have been replaced with some other realities, I'm faced with an ugly truth about myself. I will look at other people and be envious.

*Lord, I thought my problems were my body's illness
and other people. I see now that you're showing me that
the main problem is me—the inside me. How can I focus
on getting rid of that ugly part of myself?*

For personal study: 1 Kings 21:1–22

Ahab's envy leads him to disaster.

Meeting Mortality

Like an open book, you watched me grow from conception to birth;
  all the stages of my life were spread out before you,
The days of my life all prepared
  before I'd even lived one day.

*E*very sick person has heard someone, probably on more than one occasion, say, "Well, none of us knows when we'll go." The people who say this think they are identifying with the sick person; after all, we are all mortal, we're all going to die sometime. However, there is a qualitative difference between the healthy person who intellectually acknowledges her mortality and the sick person who experientially lives with her mortality. The healthy person makes plans for the future with confidence, while the sick person holds off on those plans until the next set of tests are in. That brings mortality to a place of exaggerated importance. I may not be here to celebrate my grandson's next birthday, to run around putting Christmas together, to see the bulbs I planted in the fall bloom in the spring, to even need a new winter coat. It isn't morbidity that drives such thoughts; it's reality. And this reality changes how I make decisions, how I prioritize my day, with whom I spend my time, what I do with it.

This reality forces me to live in the moment, to know that this day may be my last. The verse from Psalm 139 takes on new meaning, and I begin in a new way to request God's guidance for the day I have. Instead of worrying about who hasn't called me, why the garbage hasn't been picked up yet, or exactly where the snow-plow is when I need it, the question becomes "How can my last days be better than my first?"

I talked to an oncology nurse about the phenomenon of this dichotomy between the healthy who say, "Yes, I know I will die someday" but believe in their hearts that that day is far off, and the sick who know that "Yes, I will die soon." She said that such denial isn't limited to the healthy. When, at one training session for nurses, the patients were asked what the nurses could do to ease their situations, they said, "Don't take our hope away. Don't treat us as if we were dying." The nurse said to me, "But they are dying. What do they think is hap-pening when they see us every day for chemo, when they're swallowing morphine for pain, when they can no longer drive themselves to treatment and must arrive in

a wheelchair. Don't they realize that they are dying?"
My response was that some of the sick refuse to
acknowledge their imminent death; they think they are
fighting valiantly, while in actuality they are denying the
seriousness of their condition.

Lord, help me to see your omniscience as a comfort,
not a threat. Because you know the days of my life, because
you know me, because you love me, I can be assured that
you have my best interests in mind.

For personal study: John 11:1–44
Mary learns to trust in God.

Finding Patience

Patience is better than pride.

ECCLESIASTES 7:8 (NIV)

*T*here's a reason patients are called patients—that is something I learned in the world of the sick. Time was no longer under any part of my control. I never knew how long the fifteen-minute doctor's appointment would really take, never mind the travel time to and from the doctor's office. Sometimes it would take as long as an hour in the waiting room and another forty-five minutes in the exam room. Early in my illness, I would get antsy and cynically wonder how many patients those doctors were trying to cram into an hour. But then one day when I had waited an inordinately long amount of time, I heard the doctor go into the exam room next to mine and say to the patient, "Unfortunately, your lung cancer has returned." For the next fifteen minutes, the patient asked questions such as "How long do I have to live?" "How will I feel from now on out?""What can we do?" But I think he was entitled to those fifteen minutes. I wondered how many other, perhaps even needier patients had taken *my* time that day and many other days.

Another time, during a radiation session, an elderly man stridently questioned the nurses, "How much longer? I've been waiting over an hour." One nurse gently reminded him that he had come twenty minutes early for his appointment, so it hadn't been that long. However, they were sorry for any delay and would get to him as soon as possible. His face clouded, his jaw tightened, and his lip jutted out, showing her just how unhappy he was with her answer. Not getting any response to his mighty ruffling of feathers, the man stood up, stomped toward the door, and bitingly said over his shoulder, "I'm not waiting anymore." I wondered, since he left without his treatment, who was hurt by his stalking out: the nurses or him?

One Tuesday, I went in for my weekly chemo—something that normally took an hour and a half. The needle went into the port easily and the chemo was hiked up to a fast rate, so I hoped to be on time for school. Good. Then, about ten minutes into the faster rate, I suddenly felt as if my 150-pound Labrador had just jumped up on my left shoulder for a hug.

I motioned for the nurse to come over and told her what I was feeling. After touching the area in several different places, she declared it "boggy." "What does that mean?" I asked in a quavering voice. Responding to the tone of my voice first, she assured me that nothing terrible was going on, but I needed to have an X ray of the area to see if something was wrong with the port.

That meant going to the hospital, where the technician found that the end of the port had pulled out of my vein, causing the area to fill with saline and chemicals. That wasn't a serious situation either, but the next step was a rushed appointment with the surgeon. Of course, that entailed another car ride, yet one more waiting room, and a thirty-minute in-office surgery.

At the end of the day, including travel time, I had clocked in six hours. The Lord definitely had another plan for me that day.

Lord, I am beginning to see that I need less of me and more of you. But it's not easy to need less of me.

For personal study: Matthew 8:5–13
The centurion displays patience.

Unanswered Prayers

God, God . . . my God!
 Why did you dump me
 miles from nowhere?
Doubled up with pain, I call to God
 all the day long. No answer. Nothing.

PSALM 22:1–2

I had to have a needle biopsy when the breast cancer returned as bone cancer. There was a spot on my left, back rib, and the doctors had to determine if it was cancerous and then mark it for surgery if it was. I blithely went to the hospital, feeling fortunate that medical procedures usually didn't bother me that much. Ironically, this one bothered me plenty. I was awake for the biopsy, which I had not expected. The nurse was pleasant and chitchatted with me before the doctor came in. When he came in, I rolled onto my side as he told me and waited calmly for him to begin. He did, and the worst thing was that I felt the needle going in! *Wait a minute, God. I'm not supposed to feel any of this, am I? Stop the procedure so I can tell the doctor that I know what's going on—do something!*

The doctor did not stop, and I could feel that blasted needle all the way to my rib. *Surely you don't want me to feel this, do you, God? Where are you when I need some relief? Why aren't you listening to me? What did they do? Forget to knock me out?* The nurse was bent over me, holding my hand and arm to keep me still. I had originally considered this a comforting gesture on her part, until her hand turned into a vise when I tried to squirm away from the needle. I wasn't going anywhere, and her soothing voice, which told me we would be done soon, sounded like a rasp to my jangled nerves.

I would like to testify that the Lord miraculously stepped in and sent as many comforting angels to calm me as I needed, but he didn't. I would like to testify that all my years of Christian training came to the fore and I spouted Bible verses until my fears went away, but I didn't. I would like to testify that the tones of one of my favorite hymns came over the radio and let me know that God was with me, but no such tones came. I would like to testify that out of this spiritual low came a great spiritual high, but it didn't happen that day.

I was just happy to be finally knocked out and taken to surgery.

Lord, aid me in understanding that some days,
some experiences will be harder than others.
Let this strengthen my faith, not weaken it,
even if it doesn't seem possible at the time.

For personal study: Job 14:1–12

Job spills out his frustrations.

Stifled by Attitude

You put us on a diet of tears,
 bucket after bucket of salty tears to drink.

PSALM 80:5

One of my temptations early on in my illness was to stay focused only on myself, to filter everything through the illness, to expect everyone to give way—after all, I was sick. On one occasion, I had applied in the fall for a teaching job the next year at a college I very much wanted to work for. To that end, I asked Michigan State University to send my placement file to the college's search committee. Later, having not heard from the college, I called a friend of mine who worked there and asked if he had heard anything. He hadn't, so I waited a little longer. Meanwhile, I sent another application to a local university. Imagine my surprise when their human resources office informed me by letter that they would be glad to review my application when it was complete. The letter asked specifically for a transcript and two letters of recommendation from my graduate school professors. *What?* I wondered. *Those things should have been in my placement file already.*

I called MSU and asked the secretary to check out the file. She let me know that I was indeed missing a transcript and two letters. Somehow those pieces of information had been lost from the file. She was sorry. "Sorry," I practically hissed into the telephone. "You have cost me chances at two jobs!" All the secretary could do was repeat her apology. I was forced to ask again for recommendations. One professor dropped me a scrawled refusal that said, "So many students, so little time." I dashed off a call to my friend at the college and explained my problem. He assured me that those lapses hadn't mattered, but the committee had decided to invite two other candidates for interviews. But I knew that these lapses had mattered. I'd served on search committees before and I knew that they always looked for easy ways to weed out applications. There are simply too many applications to give people second chances.

On another occasion, I was speeding (literally) to campus in order to get to class on time. Radiation had been late that day, so I had not one moment to spare. As always, Murphy's Law applied, and a policeman stopped me. He asked me what my hurry was. I replied, "Just trying to make it to my 1:30 class," but I was thinking, *Buddy, if you try to give me a ticket, I'll pull off my wig, cry, and see if that doesn't change your mind.* Lucky for him, he didn't give me a ticket. Or lucky for me that I didn't show my temper again.

Didn't these people get it? I was sick; I deserved special treatment.

Lord, help me to not strike out at other people
when they make mistakes or when I make mistakes.
Teach me to turn my face toward you.

For personal study: 2 Kings 20:1–19
Hezekiah prays in his will, not God's.

Easing the Burdens of Others

But you, O God, are both tender and kind,
*   not easily angered, immense in love,*
*   and you never, never quit.*
So look me in the eye and show kindness,
*   give your servant the strength to go on,*
*   save your dear, dear child!*

PSALM 86:15–16

I recognized all the signs: the intent nurse seated on her stool, looking into the patient's face and talking as fast as she could while pointing to a piece of paper in her hand; the appalled friend of the patient sitting on a folding chair next to the blue Barcolounger, surreptitiously darting glances around the room at the collection of sick people in various stages of cancer; and the patient, her pupils dilated, her hands clutching the arms of the lounge, her head cocked to listen to all that the nurse was saying, her body held stiff and tight against this intrusion into her personal space, and her expression—oh, it's all you would really need to see—a mixture of suppressed terror and a plea for help.

I cautiously watched as the patient took her treatment, an IV drip that lasted about an hour. She couldn't talk to her friend, she couldn't read, she couldn't sleep, she couldn't walk. Restless to be finished, she could only sit and will herself out of there. When the chemo nurse came to take out her IV, the relief in her body and on her face was almost palpable. As the patient was leaving, I looked up at her and said, "It will get easier, I promise." Startled, she stopped for a moment, looked at my IV, and doubtfully replied, "I hope so." Studying her demeanor, I asked, "I'm not trying to be presumptuous, but may I pray for you?" "Oh, yes, my name is Sue." I've not seen Sue again, but I pray that she regularly receives comfort from God and the strength to endure what she must.

There have been too many times when I couldn't even see the others in the room. I couldn't pay attention to or have empathy for their terror. But I'm trying to learn to focus my attention on someone other than myself. Is it easy? Some days it is, but not all days. However, I believe the Lord wants me to try to ease someone else's burden.

Lord, help me pay attention to others and think about the burdens they are carrying. Let me ease someone else's grief for the day.

For personal study: Matthew 27:57–61

Joseph of Arimathea acts on his desire to help.

God Listens

Jesus wept.

John 11:35 (NIV)

*T*he shortest verse in the Bible is "Jesus wept." I remember always reciting that one as a Sunday school scholar in the race to win the badge for who had memorized the most verses. It wasn't until years later that I considered the context of that verse. Word came to Jesus that one of his good friends, Lazarus, was sick. Jesus had spent time with Lazarus and his two sisters, Mary and Martha. They had made their home available to Jesus; Mary had even anointed Jesus' feet with expensive perfume and had dried them with her hair. So these were good friends of Jesus, and I wondered why, when he heard that Lazarus was sick, Jesus waited two days before going to Bethany. Didn't Jesus know that Lazarus would die if he didn't hurry to heal him? Yes. The text is clear that Jesus understood what the delay

would mean for Lazarus, but he also understood that he needed to obey God's will so that God might be glorified. Then why did he cry when he came to their house? If he knew that he was about to perform such a wonderful act, why did he weep?

I believe he looked into the faces of Mary and Martha, saw their raw pain, and suffered with them. He didn't pat them on their arms in a comforting fashion and discount their emotion; he didn't remind them that their times were controlled by the Lord; he didn't preach to them that they should be joyful during this trial; he didn't suggest that they could be good role models to their friends and townspeople if they suffered properly. He didn't dismiss their misery; he entered into it. Even though Jesus knew that in a few moments they would be astonishingly happy, he did not disregard their experience now.

It is with such understanding that Jesus said, "In this world you will have trouble. But take heart! I have overcome the world" (John 16:33). A pastor I know described this kind of trouble as heartwrenching and desperate, but essentially momentary. Thus, I can count on my Lord's comfort and care when the medical news is bad, but I can equally count on the fact that this disease will soon be over, because God is not bound by this world, nor am I.

Lord, help me to never minimize the pain—both physical and emotional—that others are experiencing. Don't let the ready phrases escape my lips. Let me stand by my friends.

For personal study: Psalm 28:1–9

God listens.

THE LOVING SUPPORT OF FAMILY

Be careful, keep calm and don't be afraid.

ISAIAH 7:4 (NIV)

*N*ow that's good advice, but it's surely much easier to give than to follow. It's not exactly my personality to be calm, even in the happiest of circumstances. I tend to ricochet down the road of life, alternately driving on the berm and crossing the yellow line. In times of distress, though, I turn inward, and all that ricocheting goes on in my head.

Theologian Dietrich Bonhoeffer once described his grandmother as "bearing what was laid upon her, looking steadily and clearly at reality, doing whatever was required, quietly and without complaint, accepting what could not be helped." That description applies to my mother and father as well. From my first diagnosis to the last, both of them have been rock-solid strong. Less than two weeks after my mother's remaining sibling had died of brain cancer, my illness returned as brain cancer. My sister and I had talked over how to tell our parents, and we agreed that I would be as vague as possible without lying. Whatever direct questions they asked I would answer not with elaboration but with the simple truth.

I called my parents and told them that the doctor was not going to let me teach that winter because the cancer had moved again and he wanted to run some tests. I thought my mother would zero in on the teaching—she's a former teacher—but she sidestepped that and asked, "Where?"

Should I change my plan and lie? I didn't see how I could tell them the truth. It would be too much of a shock. But I did tell. Their response, "Oh, Carol, we'll pray," filled me with gratitude for their composed assurance, which I've consistently received as their daughter. My father survived non-Hodgkin's lymphoma; my mother survived breast cancer twice and two strokes. They have been models for me in taking bad news and turning it over to the Lord. That doesn't mean that they don't have emotions. When my father was diagnosed, my mother cried that she didn't want to be left behind and then got to work nursing him. During each of my mother's medical problems, my father stood beside her. I don't remember my father crying, but I do remember him giving baths, making beds, helping with therapy—all with patience. No hysterics, no sobbing—just the natural response of strong Christians: loving care.

Lord, let me appreciate more the loving support
of my family, seeing sometimes for the first time
the Christian models they are.

For personal study: 2 Timothy 1:5

Timothy learns from his grandmother and mother.

Mark 14:32–36

Jesus calls out to his Father.

When Hope Is Tried

We also rejoice in our sufferings, because we know that suffering produces perseverance; perseverance, character; and character, hope. And hope does not disappoint us, because God has poured out his love into our hearts.

Romans 5:3–5 (NIV)

I found part of this passage in Romans—the part about hope not disappointing us—comforting, but I found the context disquieting. I thought God would just *give* me hope, but no, hope comes at the end of a progression that begins with suffering. If I remain in the midst of distress without giving in to the problem, I can count on developing my character and thus developing the confidence that God will further make his presence known to me. I can see that God has something more in mind for me than just my sitting idly by, waiting for him to deposit hope in my bank account.

The cancer came back again. I had spent a month on vacation, walking and walking, declaring that I had forgotten the benefits of exercise. My leg did well, even going so far in Spain as to allow me to walk up thirty-five inclines at a prayer tower. The inclines were ramps of dirt instead of steps, made that way so that the Spaniards could ride their horses to the prayer site. I didn't have a horse, nor did anyone else, but I walked to prove to myself that I could make it. I was feeling great when I came home, ready to walk at least a mile a day to keep my legs in shape.

The morning after I got home, I was literally racing around the house, stripping beds, picking up towels, and just generally getting a jump on the day's work. I bent down to pick up the wash basket, and as I heaved it up, my back snapped. I dropped the basket, sat down for a bit, and wondered how I could have been so foolish as to twist my back. It couldn't be cancer; I'd just had a bone scan and my right side was clear. Something couldn't have come up that fast. So I swallowed some Tylenol and hobbled around gardening and cleaning anyway, knowing that I was scheduled for a bone scan the next day.

The scan showed a new lesion. Now was the time to persevere.

Lord, allow me to see that hope is not an abstract concept but a truth given through experience. Conditions I would not choose reveal hope to be muscular, not soft—real, not an idea.

For personal study: Daniel 3:8–19
Shadrach, Meshach, and Abednego hope in God.

The Mystery of Eternity

He has also set eternity in the hearts of men.

ECCLESIASTES 3:11 (NIV)

I was in for another six-month cancer checkup. I had done my chemo, my hair had grown back, and I was blithely flitting down the road of life. These six-month checkups didn't particularly bother me; in fact, when a friend was very troubled at checkup time, I told her I would pray that the Lord would send her peace, thinking to myself, *Just like he's sent me.*

I had taken the nuclear injection in the morning and was now ready for the scan. Everything was on time, so I expected to have the scan, whistle on out of the waiting room, and go on with my busy day.

Usually the technician would ask me to stay while he checked the film and then send me home. Today he said, "I need to send you down to X ray." That was the day I found out that the breast cancer had returned as bone cancer.

In reading through the Bible, I often wondered what the preacher in Ecclesiastes meant when he said, "He has set eternity in the hearts of men." Now I think he was talking about those feelings that washed over my body that day. I had a monumental desire to live, to stay here and watch my children and grandchildren grow, to enjoy life with my husband, to spend time with my extended family and friends, to complete the professional goals I had set. These visceral feelings didn't play out coolly in my mind, allowing me the distance to analyze the situation rationally and make decisions. They came as intense emotions that made my body sweat and my eyes well up with tears.

I also think the prophet was referring to my instant resistance to and disbelief in my own extinction—part of which is ego and part of which is knowledge that I was created in the divine image. While I can't explain the connection, I feel the truth of it in the resonance of God's essence and my soul. I was not created just to vanish. I am, in some mysterious way, part of eternity.

Lord, today I need a glimpse of eternity.

For personal study: Revelation 22:1–8

John tastes eternity.

A Time to Laugh

There is a time for everything . . .
a time to weep and a time to laugh.

ECCLESIASTES 3:1, 4 (NIV)

*B*y the time I had reached my third round of radiation (fifteen daily visits each round), I had gotten to know the radiation nurses very well. Their personalities ran the gamut from fairly shy to extroverted. Since I'm an extrovert myself, I was drawn to those like me, and there was a particular outdoorsy nurse with whom I kidded about a lot of things. At the end of one session, while I was still lying flat on my back, he strolled in, sniffing the air, and said, "Um-m-m. Barbecued ribs." We both laughed.

Another time, while I was waiting for a chest X ray, a woman and I struck up a conversation. I found out that she was in for one of her triweekly dialysis appointments. At one point in the conversation, she said, "I really like your hair." I quipped, "Thanks, it's a wig." With a shocked look on her face, she replied, "Girlfriend, that's not a wig!" I pulled up the edge of the wig to prove my point, and my new friend exclaimed, "Man, that looks good." In the healthy world, I couldn't joke about zapped ribs and bald heads—people would be horrified. But in the world of the sick, why not? Besides, it *is* funny.

Once, I was standing in line at a local restaurant, waiting for a friend who was meeting me for lunch. In front of me stood a woman, probably around seventy-five years old, and her son. In a heavy accent, she said to me, "Oh, I love your hair. Don't ever change it. Where I come from, we never let the damn gray hair in. You keep it like that." Privately I laughed, because indeed this hair would stay exactly the same; publicly I smiled and thanked her.

Lord, funny things happen even in illness. Don't let me lose my sense of humor or my ability to laugh at myself.

For personal study: Luke 6:21
Jesus promises that we will laugh.

Points of Terror

You will not fear the terror of night.

Psalm 91:5 (NIV)

*A*fter six years of living with cancer, I've lost count of the number of tests, procedures, and surgeries I've had. I've lost count of the number of times I've said to the Lord, "Here we are again—just you and me." In each of these situations, the Lord was always beside me, just as he promises all believers he will be. I leaned on that promise, confident as each circumstance passed that the Lord would indeed continue to make his presence known.

I don't know when a certain intolerant attitude crept into my life, but while outwardly I would cluck my tongue and sympathize with the person next to me at the clinic, inwardly I would think, *Needles terrorize you? And this is your second treatment? Just wait—there's lots of needles coming. Nausea terrorizes you? Just wait until you've tried Zofran, Compazine, Torecan—and none of them work.*

You're just beginning . . . But, of course, I never said anything; I hardly even let my mind think such thoughts.

But then, for the first time, I faced a procedure that I didn't think the Lord and I could handle. Two years ago, the cancer had struck my brain, and the treatment was a radiation series—twelve treatments in all—that involved a mask that closely fit my head and kept it still during treatment. The mask was made of mesh, and when it was heated it could be molded to my face. The technicians worked quickly, making sure I had breathing room. Then they found the site, marked it, and treated it in thirty seconds. The next eleven treatments went by quickly; my worst problem was discovering that the brand-new million-dollar machine would be down one day for tinkering.

When I went for a CT scan fifteen months later, it showed more activity in the lesion. This time around, the doctors planned to use a relatively new procedure known as an IMRT. Since my head had already been exposed to almost all the radiation it could take, the doctors would send a one-shot, intense burst of radiation to the exact location of the cancer. That meant another mask. *OK*, I thought, *Jesus and I can do that.* However, I wasn't prepared for the two new additions to the mask. First, the nurses locked it in place with three noisy and head-rattling clamps—one at the top of my head and two more above each ear. Second, the set-up time for the actual treatment, which would take place the next day, took twenty-two minutes. I know this because I asked the technician how long I had been locked down.

Only twenty-two minutes! It seemed to take at least an hour, and then I inquired how long it would take for the real treatment the next day. The technician casually said, "Oh, thirty to forty-five minutes." Stumbling out of the office, I prayed, "Well, Lord, I just can't do this. I can't even do it with your help. When they lock me in that thing, I'm a mouse caught in a trap, but I can't even wiggle my ears, nose, or whiskers." That mask fit like a second skin, so even blinking and moving my mouth were impossible. I had already used every prayer and Bible verse I could remember during the setup. I had practiced meditation, denial, distraction—anything to get through it. How would I handle the real thing? I had been scared in treatment before, but this feeling went beyond fear to terror.

I wrung my hands, I cried, I vowed to skip the treatment. As I frantically cast around for ideas, many flooded into my mind. I called my family and close friends and asked them to pray hard for me the next afternoon. I bowed my head and begged the Lord to help me meet this terror.

He sent the Twenty-third Psalm. Now, I know that's a prosaic answer, but I hadn't looked at it lately. So I went back to those beautiful words.

The LORD is my shepherd; I shall not want.
He maketh me to lie down in green pastures: he leadeth me beside
    the still waters.
He restoreth my soul: he leadeth me in the paths of righteousness for
    his name's sake.
Yea, though I walk through the valley of the shadow of death, I will
    fear no evil: for thou art *with me; thy rod and thy staff they*
    comfort me.
Thou preparest a table before me in the presence of mine enemies:
    thou anointest my head with oil; my cup runneth over.
Surely goodness and mercy shall follow me all the days of my life:
    and I will dwell in the house of the LORD for ever.

—PSALM 23 (KJV)

I recommitted the psalm to memory. The Lord graciously made it so that I did not want, I could be calm. When I walked through the valley of the shadow of death, I no longer referred to him with the distant *he*, but with the closer *thou*. At that moment, he was with me, and his rod and staff were there to comfort me. My tepid sympathy for others when they met their points of terror changed in the face of my IMRT from halfhearted to wholehearted compassion.

This time, Jesus and I didn't just go through treatment together. He took over and did for the child what she could not do for herself. He gave me a new understanding of what it means to carry my burdens to him;

he gave me an intimate experience of my relationship with him in the present.

Lord, all I can say is thank you.

For personal study: 1 Kings 19:1–9

God comforts Elijah.

TRUST

A Whole and Lasting Life

This is how much God loved the world: He gave his Son, his one and only Son. And this is why: so that no one need be destroyed; by believing in him, anyone can have a whole and lasting life.

John 3:16

This world, this time, this place is redeemed because Christ died and rose in it, souls are lost and saved here—pay attention here.

—Frederick Buechner, theologian,
from a speech at Calvin College, 1992

I'm not exactly sure when I began thinking about other people and not so much about myself, but I think it was when I decided that I needed to pray for those who were praying for me. So it was tit for tat for a while—you pray for me and I'll pray for you. Then I began to think that cancer wasn't the other patients' worst problem; being without Christ was their number one problem. So I began praying for each one's salvation, for an opportunity to speak to them about what the Lord was doing for me.

He has blessed me with many such opportunities and some stumbles too. For instance, I visited one man who nodded his thanks when I told him I was praying for him. At least, that's what I thought he was doing. When I visited him again, asking this time if I could pray out loud, he said, "No, I'm sure as hell not interested." When I visited him the third time, I didn't mention praying out loud, but I certainly was doing my share in private. He hasn't yet allowed anyone to tell him about the Lord, but I know how badly he needs to.

The Lord reminded me that it isn't only the sick who need to know him. A friend of twenty-five years came to know Jesus at a church service when she heard a sermon that was preached out of Leviticus 19. Her experience further proves that this world matters, because people are making choices every minute of their lives about where they want to spend eternity. C. S. Lewis said that the person who spends her whole life not wanting to know Jesus, resisting thoughts of heaven and service for the Lord, would be bored in heaven. We get what we want. Our Lord does not force us to follow him.

Lord, I want to spend the rest of my life with you.
Help me to understand that everyone needs that goal and
to act in such a fashion that will lead others to want
to spend their lives with you too.

For personal study: Luke 5:18–20

Others bring the paralytic man to be healed.

Angel Duties

If you stumble, they'll catch you;
their job is to keep you from falling.

PSALM 91:12

I have always been surrounded by family who have loved and prayed for me each time I've been through a new crisis. Passing the "poison" around helps, because it lightens the burden of having to carry everything by myself.

However, there was a time when I couldn't tap into my usual support system. My husband was on an overseas business trip when the doctor ordered a CT scan of my head. I decided not to call my husband home, because if everything turned out okay I would have called him home for nothing. When the CT scan showed a lesion, I decided not to call him because I could not imagine telling him such news over the telephone and having him make that trip home by himself. Since I couldn't tell him, I didn't feel it would be right to tell any other member of my family. That decision meant that I had to keep the bad news to myself for a week.

Oh, that's not true. I distinctly remember praying many times that week, "It's just you and me, Lord." Was he sufficient? Yes. But what's interesting is the way he comforted me. The nurse who called me to tell me that there was an abnormality told me the next day that she felt like a "slug" for having to tell me such news. She said that when she went home, she told her kids that someone for whom she cared deeply had gotten bad news that day and asked them if they would join her in prayer. Then she hugged me. Another nurse spent time talking with me about my decision to not call my husband home and agreed that it would be the better thing to do. The radiation doctor touched my arm when I apologized for crying and said, "Never apologize; this is a natural reaction." The oncologist, after outlining what I could expect, hugged me. So many acquaintances demonstrated God's love to me that I was overwhelmed.

I had experienced just a little taste of what some people go through, people who have no one at home to love and pray for them. And what did I find? God sends his angels in many forms to say and do the right thing, to treat patients not as diseases but as human beings who are in great need of human contact.

Lord, I need to be more like the nurse who prays
each day before coming to work to be "the hands of Jesus"
to her patients that day. I want to be your hands
to the people around me.

For personal study: Ephesians 1:15–23
Paul praises the Ephesians for their faith.

$\mathcal{W}$ALKING WITH $\mathcal{G}$OD

God, God, I'm in over my head,
Quicksand under me, swamp water over me;
I'm going down for the third time.

PSALM 69:1–2

*T*here's a song I like with a catchy tune and a snappy
rhythm. I first heard it when the cancer had come back
as a squiggly line up one of the veins in my chest wall.
As I sang along with the tape, I would consistently sing
"take me to the other side" instead of the actual lyric,
"lead me to the other side." It dawned on me that that
was what I was expecting the Lord to do—to "take" me
to the other side. After all, I didn't want to walk behind
him. That would mean I would have to do some work. I
wanted to be carried, to be rescued, to make my journey
someone else's responsibility.

Isaiah 40:31 says, "Those who hope in the Lord will
renew their strength. They will soar on wings like

eagles; they will run and not grow weary, they will walk and not be faint." A favorite preacher of mine, John Timmer, explained the verse this way: The logical progression of this verse would be the opposite—we should walk first, run second, and fly third. Why, then, did Isaiah write it this way? First, in our enthusiasm, we fly with the Spirit, filled with ecstasy that we are strong and are using that strength to perform extraordinary things. Then, we slow down a bit and run, enjoying a closeness with the Spirit beside us. Finally, something debilitating happens, and it's all we can do to walk. Our strength is spent, our physical bodies will no longer do what we want them to do, and so all we can do is walk. And we can only do that if we lean on the Lord, which is the climax of our relationship with him.

I don't save you from trouble;
I save you through trouble.
I am not so much above you,
pulling you up, as
I am beside you,
seeing you through.
I am a very present help
in trouble,
not a deliverer
out of trouble.

—JOHN TIMMER

Lord, some days I can't fly or run. Teach me
that walking too will bring me closer to you.
Life is not a competition but a completion.
That completion is what I need to concentrate on.

For personal study: Philippians 3:7–14

Paul endures.

Tests of Faith

*The reason I wrote you was to see if you would stand the
test and be obedient in everything.*

2 Corinthians 2:9 (NIV)

I was now a regular at the clinic, having been there
for five sets of chemo over six years. I had been poked,
prodded, and stuck with IV needles in either my veins
or my port and had gotten used to the routine—or so I
thought. One day I went in for my weekly chemo and
jokingly said to the nurse, "On a scale of one to ten for
pain, one being the lowest and ten being the highest, IV
needles rank about a one." We laughed, and she began
searching for a good vein. Luckily, the veins on my right
side were still pretty good, and since I had been having
weekly injections for more than a year, I didn't think
much about what was happening.

The nurse missed on the first try, apologized, and
began looking for another vein. She found one and tried

again. This one didn't work either. One of the unwritten rules of the clinic is that a nurse will replace herself after two attempts to get an IV started. My nurse did that, and another nurse came over. The replacement nurse searched for a vein, found one, and tried again. No luck! So she bent to her work again, found another spot, and poked. Even though she stayed in that spot working the needle around to find the vein, she was unsuccessful too. She felt terrible. I didn't know why she felt so bad; it was my hand. But I didn't say that to her. That was four unsuccessful tries, something that had never happened to me before. We were forty minutes into the process, and it was bringing up ugly memories of the nurses' attempts the previous week to find a suitable vein on another woman, whom they worked on for more than an hour.

I was praying like mad for the needle to find a vein, but something else was going on too. I had many times witnessed to those around me about my faith in Jesus; the nurses too knew that I claimed to be a Christian. But I wasn't feeling very Christian at the moment. This was no longer a minor occurrence, and I was getting angry at the nurses, wondering why I should have two incompetent ones in a row. I wanted to say something sarcastic to them; I wanted them to know that I didn't think this was funny at all. But I managed to hold my tongue—just barely.

Another nurse came by and explained that the clinic was using new needles, so perhaps that was the reason they were having such a hard time. That was an explanation I didn't want to hear! I stayed quiet, thinking the Lord would surely reward me with success this fifth time. He did not, and the look in the nurse's eyes told me how upset she was. She was upset? What did she think I was?

On the sixth try, the nurse was successful. Then all three nurses surrounded me and told me how much they appreciated my attitude during this ordeal. I was grateful that I had not given in to the temptation to tell them what I was thinking.

Lord, I don't like tests, but I love you. Help me demonstrate that to the people around me.

For personal study: Acts 16:19–28
Paul and Silas sing in prison.

Close to God's Heart

He gathers the lambs in his arms
and carries them close to his heart.

Isaiah 40:11 (NIV)

*T*here are times in our lives when we too need such a shepherd. The cancer had metastasized again, this time to a major organ. When my doctor gave me the news, he said, "Most succumb to this in six to nine months." That number wasn't very promising, so I tried to put myself in a holding pattern, counting on the Lord for grace while I waited to see if the radiation would help. However, that's hard to do, and for the two months I had to wait I found myself planning my funeral and praying that the Lord would take me quickly. I had to take another battery of tests so those results could be compared with the earlier test results. Then I had to wait for yet another week to go by.

The Sunday before the weeklong wait our pastor preached on walking with God. In order to make his point visual, he carried his ten-month-old son in a backpack throughout his sermon. At one point, our pastor related the story of an early morning walk he had taken with his son during summer vacation. In the beginning of the walk, the day was crisp and beautiful, but when they were at the farthest point from home, it began to rain, so lightly at first that his son thought the new experience was fun. When it began to rain harder and his son found himself soaked, he began to cry. Lightning flashed and winds whipped around them, terrifying the child so much that he screamed out to his father for help. At that point in the story, our pastor sat down, carefully took his son out of the backpack, stood up, and held him close to his heart, crooning, "It's okay. We're gonna make it home. I love you."

That picture of God stayed with me all week as I imagined God holding me close to his heart when I faced frightening storms and soothing me when I recognized how much I needed his comfort. Suddenly, it didn't look like weakness to cry out to God and tell him how scared I was. Suddenly, it didn't look like distrust if I cried out my dread to him.

Lord, why don't I come to you sooner rather than later?
You're always there when I admit my desperate need for you.

For personal study: 2 Kings 4:8–37

Elisha responds to the Shunammite's pleas.

Accepting God's Will

*"My friend Job will pray for you, and I will accept his prayer. He will ask me not to treat you as you deserve."...
And God accepted Job's prayer.*

Job 42:8–9

Why did Job have to pray for those miserable friends of his? I've begun to think about that. I used to think that he probably just did it because that's what God commanded him to do. "Oh, all right. If that's what you want, I will, I suppose." But now I'm not so sure. I think Job learned something about God's will as he traveled along the road of physical disability. Perhaps he learned that he had to decide whether to do God's will with a generous heart or with a begrudging one. That reminds me of Jonah. Was there anyone else in the Bible who fought the Lord's will for his life quite like Jonah? Now, you'd think a shipwreck and three days in the belly of a fish would have changed his mind, and it did, sort of.

He preached well enough—he must have worked at it—to see a great revival. Or maybe he did only a half-hearted job, but God honored his word and still sent a revival. The point is that it was God's will that those Ninevites have a chance to repent. Remember Jonah's reaction when they did? "This is why I ran to Tarshish! Oh, didn't I just know you were a kind and forgiving God who wants to show mercy? Didn't I just know you'd do this?" Madeleine L'Engle, who wrote *The Journey with Jonah,* imagines God replying to Jonah with a question: "Do you think it's easier to forgive than destroy?" The answer most times for we humans is no; it's much easier to destroy than forgive. After all, you have wronged *me*, and I won't let you get away with that!

But surely it's easier for God to forgive! He's in the forgiving business, I used to think. I believe he does forgive, but I no longer believe it's so easy. I say, "Sorry, Lord" and go cheerfully on my way, secure in his promises of forgiveness. But have I ever taken a moment to reflect on the fact that I have been responsible for grieving the heart of God? I know he's not surprised by anything I say or do, and I know my sin makes him angry, but grieve him? Now that's something both Jonah and I need to think about. We can say, "Okay. I'll do it your way. After all, I have to, don't I?" Or we can say with sincerity what Jonah hurled at God in anger, "I knew that you are a gracious and compassionate God, slow to anger and abounding in love, a God who relents from sending calamity" (Jonah 4:2). It must have been with this attitude that Job prayed for his friends. Joyful responses to difficult situations are possible.

Lord, sometimes living out your plan for my life is tedious, and sometimes it seems as if I can't do what you ask. Give me the understanding that will make it possible for me to accept what I honestly desire—your will for my life.

For personal study: Esther 4:10–17; 5:1–8
Esther finds the strength to help her people.

Living with Illness

I don't battle cancer; I dislike that metaphor. War would take all my time and energy. I would have to determine how many and what kinds of troops I had and what provisions headquarters had sent. I would have to labor over a battle plan, right down to identifying an avenue for retreat, and then I would have to fight. That would mean charging ahead, firing my weapon, keeping my platoon leader in sight, helping a fallen comrade, ducking for cover, winning or losing that battle, and getting ready to fight again. In fact, if I were a good soldier, all my time and thoughts would be consumed with the battle at hand.

I have a friend who behaves like that. Actually, he doesn't have cancer, but his wife does—brain cancer. She will be the second wife he will have lost to brain cancer. He's angry—with the doctors, the disease, God. He fights hard to find the right doctors in both conventional and alternative medicine. He shakes his fist at God, declaring him unfair. His tense body language and the strident tone of his voice bespeak a man in full battle regalia. He *will* win, he *will* "beat this thing," if it's the last thing he does.

I simply refuse to give cancer that high of a priority in my life. Rather, I prefer to live with cancer. That's not to say that I don't find the best doctors, but when I do, I trust their treatment plans rather than shop around for the top five "plans of attack." And while I'm not happy to have cancer, I don't see it as a monster ready to pounce on me when I let down my guard. I can't say that I don't complain to God about his plan for me—I do—but I know from the assurances of his Spirit in me that I will find hope in knowing that God, not this ephemeral world, is the ground of my existence. Yes, I have been in a waiting room, and on a gurney, and hooked up to chemo, but I could still think about other things and talk to those around me. I don't have to go through my life wearing battle fatigues. I can live.

Lord, let me learn that your ways are perfect. Let me rely more on the knowledge I already have about you. Let me count the ways in which you have already blessed me.

For personal study: Judges 16:23–30
Samson follows the Lord.

Everything Bright
and Beautiful

We pray that you'll have the strength to stick it out over the long haul—not the grim strength of gritting your teeth but the glory-strength God gives. It is strength that endures the unendurable and spills over into joy, thanking the Father who makes us strong enough to take part in everything bright and beautiful that he has for us.

Colossians 1:11–12

When my mother was diagnosed with breast cancer the second time, she called me and said, "I just wish I could go away, have this done, and not tell anybody." Many years later, she fell and broke her right elbow. That time she said, "I thought as I hit the floor, 'What have I done to my family now?'" I didn't really understand those two statements until recently.

When my breast cancer came back as bone cancer, I too hated to think about telling my family. Then it came back again as breast cancer, and I dreaded the telling worse. When it ran up one of my left chest veins and into the lymph nodes around my neck, I cried at the thought of facing everyone yet again. When it reappeared as brain cancer, it seemed impossible to tell them about this latest downturn. The thought of watching my beloved husband's face crumple and his eyes well up with tears made my stomach knot. Add to that telling my children, my parents, my sister, and my friends, and I knew experientially what my mother meant when she said, "What have I done to my family now?" The desire to save them any more pain, to stave off their grieving, was so strong that I didn't know how to deal with it.

The passage from Colossians has been my guidepost for several years. God has at every turn given me strength to endure what the illness brings. Over time, he has even turned my attitude from stoicism to joy, grounded here by family and friends and in heaven by Jesus Christ himself. However, the last phrase—"to take part in everything bright and beautiful that he has for us"—consistently confused me. Surely illness can't be "bright and beautiful." Okay, maybe "bright" could mean attention getting, and illness is that. In fact, once I truly focused my attention on the illness, I saw that it put other things into perspective; it wasn't that the illness got all the attention, but it became a filter to help me discern what mattered and what didn't.

"Beautiful" continued to elude me. Beautiful? How? The illness was ugly, the treatments were difficult, and the side effects were often debilitating. But once I took my eyes off the illness, they rested naturally on those around me. And I saw that "beautiful" would indeed describe the love given to me by my husband, characterized by prayer, steadfastness, and assurance; the love showered on me by my daughter and her family; the love of my praying parents; the love of my sister, characterized by her willingness to share in my daily struggles; and the love of my friends.

Lord, allow me to discern the difference between dogged obedience and joyful obedience. Mostly, if I can stop thinking about myself and begin to really see others, I can be joyful.

For personal study: Acts 5:17–32
The apostles stand firm.

Focusing on God

You made me like a handcrafted piece of pottery—
and now are you going to smash me to pieces?

Job 10:8

*O*ne of the hardest parts of having a long-lasting illness is accepting, even embracing, that the suffering comes from God. I know that he has the power to turn it away from me, so why doesn't he choose to do that? Like Job, I certainly don't claim to be sinless. But also like Job, I know that I'm not an apostate. In fact, I've tried hard to love God, and I wonder why my life is going like this. On a human level, I can watch people all around me get sick and die. I can piously mutter platitudes to them, such as "All things work together for good for those who love the Lord" and "The Lord is in control; everything will be okay." But when it comes my turn, I'm shocked. I touch my body to reassure myself that it's still there; I listen to my heart to make sure it hasn't stopped. Why I am shocked by physical illness, I have no idea, but I am.

This is why I think that praying for healing is not the best thing to do. Of course, in the beginning of my illness I prayed for healing. But as the years have passed, I've stopped praying for healing; rather, I pray for God's best will in my life, because in doing so I agree to be obedient to him, with or without healing. Then, instead of focusing on myself, I can focus on him.

I've read about Jesus' night in Gethsemane. I know his agony was so physical and emotional that he sweat great drops of blood. He begged his Father to take death away from him, but God did not, because his plan for Jesus' life was to redeem the sin of the world. I know that while his plan for me is nothing so grandiose, he does have one. Will I know what it is while I'm on earth? Probably not. Will I have my questions answered? Probably not. In fact, it occurs to me that when I am able to ask him any question I want and get his answer, I won't even want to bother. When I stand before him and see him, when I'm in my resurrection body instead of this old, creaky one, I will want only to fall on my face in worship. Finally, my ego will be gone, and all that will remain will be the part of me that is made in his image and makes me unique. We're not told what Moses and Elijah looked like on the mount of the Transfiguration, but they were recognizable.

What disappeared for them, and what will disappear for me, is that grasping, selfish, me-first part. Somehow I don't think it will be so important for the new me to have my earthly questions answered.

Lord, today I need a spiritual boost that will assure me that only ultimate things matter and that you are in charge. I put my confidence in you.

For personal study: Philippians 1:12–22
Paul puts the gospel above everything else.

Clay Jars

But we have this treasure in jars of clay to show that this all-surpassing power is from God and not from us. We are hard pressed on every side, but not crushed; perplexed, but not in despair; persecuted, but not abandoned; struck down, but not destroyed. We always carry around in our body the death of Jesus, so that the life of Jesus may also be revealed in our body.

2 Corinthians 4:7–10 (NIV)

*I*n biblical times, people put their valuables in the clay jars they used around their houses so that thieves wouldn't be able to find them. After all, what self-respecting thief would put his hand in a garbage jar thinking he might find gold, or dig around in a flower pot whose plant had turned into dead sticks, or take down that old cracked, dusty pot to see what was inside. And yet, that's what Corinthians promises God did. He put the gospel in humans in order to show that any beauty found there comes from him.

When I look around the chemo room, I see a woman who has been oppressed by the indignity of having no hair, yet isn't crushed in spirit. She can still lift her eyes, smile at the nurse, and thank her for the good job she did starting the IV. I see a man perplexed by having to wear a device that will dispense chemo around the clock. He must feel hopeless, and yet I see that he is not in total despair. After the nurses show him how to operate his mechanical device, he gives it a test run and shoots a thumbs-up signal to the room. I see the pitiful specter of a man who is so thin and gray that I wonder how he can function at all. And yet when the nurse asks, "Which hand shall we start the IV on today?" he can still joke by lifting both his arms a little and replying, "Your choice." I see a man in a private chemo room, so obviously thrown down by the disease that he can only raise a finger in greeting when his wife comes into the room. But he does that. Are these frail jars of clay? Yes. Are they containers for the hope of resurrection? Yes.

Lord, thank you for giving me evidence of your true self. Thank you for using others and me for that purpose.

For personal study: Acts 7:6–15, 51–60

Stephen sees heaven.

A Well-Watered Place

Didn't he set us on the road to life?
   Didn't he keep us out of the ditch?
He trained us first,
   passed us like silver through refining fires,
Brought us into hardscrabble country,
   pushed us to our very limit,
Road-tested us inside and out,
   took us to hell and back;
Finally he brought us
   to this well-watered place.

PSALM 66:9–12

This passage reminds me of Romans 8:28, "That's why we can be so sure that every detail in our lives of love for God is worked into something good"—the verse I so disliked at the beginning of my journey with illness. Now I've grown a little bit, and I can see illness from an evolving perspective. I'm trying to learn to let go of control and to trust the one who keeps me out of the ditch of hopelessness. I'm trying to learn that discipline is not negative, but the work of God, who made me and knows what final product he has in mind. I'm trying to learn not to fear the fire but to treasure any help it gives in burning away forever the dross of selfishness from my life. I'm trying to learn to love the hardscrabble country *for* its harshness. We who travel there find that it has beauty only a trained inner eye can see. I'm trying to learn that my physical, emotional, and spiritual limits are wider and broader than my original, comfortable world could have ever shown me. I'm trying to learn that road testing, while it seems unnecessary to see how fast I can go from zero to sixty or if the heater works well, has a purpose for the designer of the vehicle. I'm trying to learn that my descent into hell can be an illustration for others who must travel the same route, and I'm trying to show others who watch from a distance that even in hell God is with me.

I have learned that every moment of every day can be a well-watered place if I obediently turn my will over to my heavenly Father. I can't learn these lessons in an episode of illness or even in a lifetime of illness, but I can glimpse their meanings and worth with greater surety as the journey continues. "The son of God suffered unto death not that men might not suffer, but that their sufferings might be like his" (George

Macdonald). This is a high standard; I need daily help in trying to reach for it.

Lord, I am beginning to understand that I will never know completely why you do what you do or what every circumstance means. But your expectations are not beyond my reach. Keep me striving.

For personal study: John 16:4–14

Jesus sends us his Holy Spirit to guide us into truth and light.

RESOURCES

Here are a few resources to help you explore in depth the ideas in *When Hope Is Tried*.

The Journey of the Mind to God
Bonaventure (edited by Stephen F. Brown, translated by Philotheus Boehner, O.F.M.)
Hackett Publishing Company

The Cost of Discipleship
Dietrich Bonhoeffer (translated by R. H. Fuller)
Macmillan

I and Thou
Martin Buber (translated by Walter Kaufmann)
Scribner

Honey from the Rock
Lawrence Kushner
Jewish Lights Publishing

Christian Reflections
C. S. Lewis (edited by Walter Hooper)
William B. Eerdmans Publishing

Till We Have Faces: A Myth Retold
C. S. Lewis
Harcourt, Brace

Conjectures of a Guilty Bystander
Thomas Merton
Doubleday

I Want to Be a Christian
J. I. Packer
Tyndale House Publishers

*The Divine Conspiracy: Rediscovering Our
   Hidden Life in God*
Dallas Willard
HarperSanFrancisco

Spiritual Disciplines for the Christian Life
Donald S. Whitney
NavPress

The Gift of Peace

Personal Reflections

by Joseph Cardinal Bernardin

"A gem of a book, reminiscent of the best of Henri Nouwen ..."

Publishers Weekly

$17.95 Hardcover
ISBN: 0-8294-0955-6

*I*n the final two months of his life, Joseph Cardinal Bernardin made it his mission to share his personal reflections and insights in *The Gift of Peace*. Using as a framework the previous three years, which included a widely publicized false accusation of sexual misconduct, a diagnosis of cancer, and the return of the cancer after fifteen months of remission, Cardinal Bernardin tells his story openly and honestly. At the end of his life, the cardinal was at peace. He accepted his peace as a gift from God, and through this book, he shares that gift with us all.

LOYOLAPRESS. 3441 N. Ashland Ave. Chicago, IL 60657
www.loyolapress.org

To order, call 800-621-1008 or fax 773-281-0555